Table of Contents

Introduction

Welcome to "The Ultimate Guide on How to Start a Music Production Business." If you're here, you're probably dreaming of turning your love for music into a thriving business. Well, you've come to the right place! This guide is packed with all the essential information and strategies you need to launch and grow your own music production business successfully.

In this guide, we'll dive deep into every aspect of starting a music production business. We'll cover everything from assessing your skills and resources, understanding your target market, developing your services and pricing, to setting up your studio and equipment. We'll also walk you through the legal and business considerations, marketing and promotion strategies, and how to acquire clients and build lasting relationships. Plus, we'll explore how to provide exceptional service and quality, and ultimately, how to grow your music production business.

Whether you're a music enthusiast eager to turn your passion into profit or someone with professional experience in the industry, this guide has got you covered. We're here to equip you with the knowledge and insights to navigate the complexities of the music production business.

Starting a music production business is an exhilarating and rewarding endeavor. You'll get to contribute to the creative process, collaborate with talented artists, and play a crucial role in shaping the sound of various projects. However, like any entrepreneurial venture, it requires careful planning, strategic decision-making, and hard work to succeed.

Throughout this book, each chapter is dedicated to a specific aspect of starting and running a music production business. By the time you finish, you'll have a comprehensive understanding of the key considerations and actionable steps necessary to build a successful music production business.

So, if you're ready to embark on this exciting journey, let's dive in and explore the world of music production together. Get comfortable, grab a cup of coffee, and let's get started on turning your dream into reality!

Chapter 1: Introduction to the Music Production Business

Welcome to the exciting world of music production! This industry is a thrilling and rewarding space where you can transform your passion for music into a profitable business venture. With technology becoming more accessible and the ever-growing demand for high-quality music, starting a music production business has never been more viable. Whether you're a musician, audio engineer, or just someone with a keen interest in music, this chapter will give you a comprehensive understanding of what it takes to get started and succeed in the music production business.

The Role of a Music Production Business

A music production business is at the heart of creating and delivering music projects. It encompasses a variety of activities, including recording and mixing tracks, producing albums, composing and arranging music, and providing sound engineering services. These businesses collaborate closely with artists, bands, record labels, and other industry professionals to bring their creative visions to life. They are crucial in ensuring that the final product meets the highest standards of sound quality and artistic integrity.

The Benefits of Starting a Music Production Business

Starting a music production business comes with several enticing benefits, especially for those passionate about music and sound. Here are some key advantages:

1. **Creative Expression:** As a music producer, you'll have the chance to work closely with artists and collaborate on a wide range of exciting projects. Your unique skills and creativity will play a vital role in shaping the final product, helping to bring out the best in the music.

2. **Flexibility and Independence:** Running your own music production business gives you the freedom to choose your clients, projects, and working hours. This flexibility allows you to pursue projects that align with your interests and goals, helping you maintain a healthy work-life balance.

3. **Lucrative Career Opportunities:** The demand for music production services is on the rise, creating numerous career opportunities in the industry. With the right skills and a solid reputation, you can attract high-paying clients and establish yourself as a respected professional.

4. **Personal Satisfaction:** There's a profound sense of satisfaction that comes from watching your clients' music come to life and receiving recognition for your work. Helping artists achieve their goals and creating memorable music can be incredibly rewarding.

5. **Growth Potential:** With a strong foundation and a network of connections, your music production business has the potential to expand and grow over time. As you gain expertise and establish your brand, you can take on larger projects, build a team, and explore new avenues within the music industry.

The Challenges of Starting a Music Production Business

While the music production business offers numerous benefits, it's essential to be aware of the challenges you might face. Here are some common hurdles:

1. **Initial Investment:** Setting up a music production studio requires a significant investment in equipment, software, and acoustic treatment. It's crucial to budget appropriately and ensure you have the necessary resources to provide high-quality services.
2. **Competition:** The music production industry is highly competitive, with many talented professionals vying for clients and projects. To succeed, you need to differentiate yourself by offering unique services, building a strong portfolio, and delivering exceptional quality.
3. **Building a Client Base:** Acquiring clients can be challenging, especially when you're just starting. Building relationships and effectively marketing your services are

essential for attracting clients and generating a steady stream of projects.

4. **Evolving Technology:** The music production industry is constantly evolving, with new technologies and software being introduced regularly. Staying up-to-date with the latest trends and tools is crucial to remain competitive and deliver the best results for your clients.

Starting a music production business requires a blend of passion, technical skills, and business acumen. By understanding the role of a music production business and being aware of its benefits and challenges, you can embark on a rewarding entrepreneurial journey in the fascinating world of music production. Let's dive deeper into the details and explore how you can turn your musical dreams into reality!

Chapter 2: Assessing Your Skills and Resources

When you're gearing up to start a music production business, taking a good look at your skills and resources is key. This self-assessment will help you pinpoint where you shine and where you might need a little boost. By understanding both your strengths and your limitations, you can build a strong foundation for your business and make informed decisions that will lead to your success.

Evaluating Your Skills

First things first, let's dive into your musical and technical abilities. As a music producer, it's crucial to have a solid grasp of music theory, composition, and arrangement. You should also be proficient in using various music production software and equipment. Take a moment to honestly inventory your abilities. Are there areas where you feel super confident? Are there others where you might need some improvement? If you spot any gaps in your knowledge or skills, don't worry. Consider taking some courses, attending workshops, or finding a mentor to help you level up. The more well-rounded and knowledgeable you are, the more value you'll bring to your clients.

Assessing Your Technical Resources

Now, let's talk about the technical side of things. What kind of equipment, software, and studio space do you have access to? Make a comprehensive list of your technical resources, including audio interfaces, microphones, speakers, headphones, and software plugins. Take a close look at the quality and capabilities of your existing gear. Does it match up with the services you want to offer? If you find that your equipment might need some upgrades or if you need additional tools to meet the demands of your target market, it's time to budget for those expenses. Investing in the right equipment can make a huge difference in the quality of your work and the satisfaction of your clients.

Recognizing Your Personal and Professional Network

Your resources aren't just about gear and software; they also include your personal and professional network. Networking is a crucial part of running a successful music production business. Referrals and word-of-mouth recommendations can play a significant role in acquiring clients. Think about your connections within the music industry. Do you know musicians, artists, producers, engineers, or other industry professionals who might be able to collaborate with you or refer clients to your business? Building and nurturing these relationships can be incredibly valuable for your business's growth and success.

Identifying Financial Resources

Starting a music production business also requires some financial investment. Assess your financial resources to determine how much capital you have available for things like equipment, studio rental, marketing, and other business expenses. Do you have personal savings to dip into, or will you need to secure external funding through loans or investors? Creating a budget and financial plan that covers both your initial startup costs and ongoing operational expenses is essential. This will help you make informed decisions about pricing your services and managing your finances effectively.

Conclusion

Assessing your skills and resources is a critical step in starting your music production business. By understanding where you excel and where you might need some help, you can develop strategies to leverage your strengths and overcome any challenges. Take the time to evaluate your technical abilities, personal and professional network, and financial resources. This will give you a solid foundation to build your music production business on.

Chapter 3: Understanding Your Target Market

Hey there! Let's dive into one of the most crucial aspects of running a successful music production business: understanding your target market. By really getting to know the people you want to serve, you can tailor your services, marketing strategies, and pricing to perfectly match their needs and preferences. So, how do you go about identifying your target market? It all starts with some good old-fashioned market research.

Defining Your Ideal Customer

First things first, you need to create a detailed profile of your ideal customer. Picture them in your mind: how old are they? What's their gender? Where do they live? What kind of music do they love? Think about their specific needs or challenges. By doing this, you can focus your efforts on a particular group of people who are most likely to be interested in what you have to offer.

Conducting Market Research

Next up, it's time to gather some information. This involves using various research methods like online surveys, interviews with potential customers, and diving into data from industry reports and publications. Look for trends, preferences, and gaps in the market. This will help you understand what people are looking for and where there might be opportunities for your business to step in.

Analyzing Competition

Take a good look at your competition. Who are they targeting? How do they position themselves in the industry? By studying them, you can find underserved segments or identify unique selling points that can set your music production business apart from the rest.

Identifying Key Influencers

In the music world, influencers play a big role. These are people who have a significant impact on the decisions of artists, producers, and record labels. Identify these key influencers and get to know their preferences and needs. Building relationships with them can help you gain credibility and attract more clients.

Segmenting Your Market

Once you've gathered all your data and insights, it's time to segment your target market. Break it down into smaller groups based on common characteristics or needs. This way, you can create targeted marketing campaigns and develop specialized services for each segment.

Developing Personas

Now, let's make it even more tangible by developing personas. These are fictional characters that represent different segments of your target market. Create detailed personas that include information about their demographics, preferences, goals, challenges, and how your music production services can help them. These personas will guide your marketing and communication efforts, making everything feel more personalized and relevant.

Fine-tuning Your Messaging

With a clear understanding of your target market, you can craft compelling messages that truly resonate with them. Highlight the unique benefits and value proposition of your music production services. Show them how you can solve their specific challenges or help them achieve their musical aspirations.

Keep Evolving

Remember, understanding your target market isn't a one-time thing. As the music industry evolves and customer preferences change, it's important to stay updated and adapt your strategies accordingly. Regularly review and analyze market data to ensure that your music production business stays relevant and continues to attract and serve your target market effectively.

By following these steps and continuously learning about your target market, you'll be in a great position to tailor your services and marketing efforts to meet their needs. This will not only help you stand out in the competitive music industry but also build a loyal customer base that trusts and values your expertise. Happy researching!

Chapter 4: Developing Your Services and Pricing

Let's dive into one of the most crucial steps in starting your music production business: developing your services and pricing. This involves figuring out exactly what services you'll offer and how you'll price them. This chapter will walk you through creating services that meet your target market's needs and establishing competitive pricing to ensure your business thrives.

Understanding Your Target Market's Needs

Before you start developing your services, you need to understand your target market's needs and preferences deeply. Conducting market research is key here. Gather insights about the types of music production services that are in demand. This will help you spot gaps and opportunities you can take advantage of.

Also, consider specific niches within the music industry you can cater to. Are you interested in working with independent artists, bands, or record labels? Understanding your target market will allow you to tailor your services to their unique requirements. The more you know about what your potential clients need, the better you can serve them.

Identifying Your Core Services

Once you've got a good grasp on your target market, it's time to identify your core services. These are the main offerings you'll provide to your clients. Common music production services include recording, mixing, mastering, composing, and sound design.

Think about your skills, experience, and technical capabilities when deciding which services to offer. Focus on areas where you have expertise and can deliver exceptional results. Providing specialized services can help you stand out from the competition and attract clients who value your unique skills.

Diversifying Your Service Offerings

While having core services is important, diversifying your offerings can help you expand your client base and increase your revenue streams. Think about additional services you can provide that complement your core offerings. For example, you could offer music production consultations, song arrangement and production, or even music licensing services.

Diversification allows you to cater to different client needs and reach a wider audience. It also positions you as a comprehensive solution provider in the music production industry.

Pricing Your Services Strategically

Determining the right pricing for your services is crucial to ensure profitability while staying competitive in the market. Here are some factors to consider when setting your prices:

1. **Market Rates:** Research the typical prices charged by other music production businesses in your area or niche. This will give you a benchmark to work with and help you position your pricing competitively.
2. **Your Expertise and Experience:** If you have extensive experience or specialized skills, you can justify charging higher rates. Highlight your qualifications and expertise when discussing pricing with potential clients.
3. **Overhead Costs:** Consider the costs associated with running your business, such as equipment maintenance, studio rent, and software subscriptions. Take these expenses into account when determining your rates to ensure you cover your overhead costs.
4. **Value Offered:** Focus on the value you provide to your clients rather than solely competing on price. Showcase the quality of your work, customer satisfaction, and the overall experience you provide. Clients are often willing to pay more for exceptional service and results.
5. **Packages and Bundles:** Consider offering different packages or bundled services to cater to different client needs and budgets. This allows clients to choose

options that best suit their requirements and increases your potential for upselling.

6. **Profit Margin:** Ensure that your pricing allows for a healthy profit margin. Factor in your desired income and business growth goals when setting your rates.

Remember, pricing isn't set in stone. Regularly assess and adjust your pricing strategy based on market trends, client feedback, and changes in your business expenses.

Conclusion

Developing your services and pricing strategy is a vital part of starting a music production business. By aligning your services with the needs of your target market and pricing them strategically, you can attract clients, differentiate yourself from competitors, and achieve profitability. Continuously evaluate and refine your services and pricing to ensure you meet the evolving demands of the music industry.

So, take the time to plan out your services and pricing carefully. It's a crucial step that can set the foundation for your business's success. Good luck!

Chapter 5: Setting Up Your Studio and Equipment

Setting up your studio and acquiring the necessary equipment is a pivotal step in starting a music production business. The quality of your studio and equipment will directly impact the quality of your work and the satisfaction of your clients. In this chapter, we'll dive into the key considerations and steps involved in setting up your studio and acquiring the right equipment, all while keeping things practical and approachable.

Designing Your Studio Space

First things first, you need to design an optimal workspace that meets your specific needs. Here are some key factors to consider:

Acoustics: Your studio's acoustics are crucial. Good acoustic treatment will minimize unwanted noise and reflections, giving you a clean, balanced sound. Think about using soundproofing materials, diffusers, and absorbers to get the best results. This step might seem technical, but it's all about creating an environment where you can hear your music accurately.

Layout: A well-thought-out layout can make a huge difference in your workflow. Arrange your equipment, monitoring speakers, and workstations in a way that allows for easy movement and enhances efficiency. You want a setup that's ergonomic and functional, so you can focus on being creative without unnecessary hassles.

Comfort: Don't underestimate the importance of comfort. Invest in quality furniture, proper lighting, and climate control to create a pleasant environment for yourself and your clients. A comfortable studio is a productive studio, and it can make long hours of work much more enjoyable.

Essential Equipment

To run a music production business, you'll need a range of essential equipment. Let's break down the key pieces:

Computers: Your computer is the heart of your studio. Invest in a powerful system capable of handling the demands of music production software. Look for a computer with robust processing power, plenty of RAM, and ample storage capacity.

Audio Interface: The audio interface is the bridge between your computer and external audio devices. It converts analog audio signals into digital data and vice versa. Choose an interface that offers high-quality sound conversion and has enough input and output options for your needs.

Microphones: A variety of microphones is essential for different recording situations. Dynamic microphones are great for vocals and instruments, condenser microphones excel in studio settings, and ribbon microphones can provide a vintage sound. Having a selection gives you flexibility and better results.

Headphones and Monitors: High-quality monitoring equipment, including headphones and studio monitors, is crucial. Look for gear with a flat frequency response and accurate sound reproduction. This ensures precise mixing and mastering, helping you make the best decisions for your projects.

Software: Professional digital audio workstations (DAWs) and plugins are the backbone of your music production capabilities. Research and invest in industry-standard software that suits your workflow and creative needs. This is where a lot of the magic happens, so choose tools that you're comfortable with and that inspire you.

Additional Equipment

In addition to the essentials, you might need some extra gear to enhance your setup:

MIDI Controllers: MIDI controllers provide a tactile and expressive way to interact with your software and instruments. Keyboards, drum pads, and control surfaces can greatly enhance your workflow and creativity.

Outboard Gear: Consider adding outboard gear like compressors, equalizers, and effects processors to your setup. These can add analog warmth and character to your recordings, offering more creative options and improving your overall sound.

Instruments and Sample Libraries:
Depending on the services you offer, you may need a variety of musical instruments or sample libraries to create different styles and genres of music. Think about the specific needs of your target market and invest accordingly.

Research and Budget

Before making any purchases, conduct thorough research. Read reviews, seek recommendations from trusted sources, and test out equipment whenever possible. Creating a budget is also crucial to determine how much you can allocate for your studio setup and equipment purchases. This ensures you're making informed decisions and staying within your financial limits.

Upgrades and Maintenance

Remember, your studio setup and equipment will require regular upgrades and maintenance to keep up with advancements in technology and ensure optimal performance. Stay informed about new software releases, hardware advancements, and industry trends. Regularly updating and maintaining your equipment will help you provide the best possible service to your clients and keep your studio running smoothly.

Conclusion

Setting up your studio and acquiring the right equipment is vital for running a successful music production business. Focus on designing your studio space with acoustics, comfort, and workflow in mind. Invest in essential equipment like computers, audio interfaces, microphones, headphones, and software. Consider additional gear like MIDI controllers, outboard equipment, and instruments based on your needs. Conduct thorough research, create a budget, and stay updated on upgrades and maintenance to ensure the longevity and quality of your studio setup. With these steps, you'll be well on your way to creating a professional and productive music production environment.

Chapter 6: Legal and Business Considerations

Starting a music production business is about much more than just creating amazing tracks. It's essential to grasp the legal and business aspects to ensure your enterprise thrives in the music industry. In this chapter, we will delve into the various legal and business considerations you need to be aware of and address when starting your music production business.

Protecting Your Intellectual Property

When you create music, safeguarding your intellectual property rights is crucial. Copyright law grants exclusive rights to the creator of an original work, including musical compositions and sound recordings. Registering your work with the appropriate copyright authorities provides legal protection and enables you to enforce your rights if someone infringes upon them. Consulting with an intellectual property attorney can help you navigate the complexities of copyright law and ensure your music is properly protected. They can assist you in registering your works, drafting licensing agreements, and advising you on handling any infringement disputes that may arise.

Business Structure and Licensing

Choosing the right business structure for your music production business is vital for legal and tax purposes. Common options include sole proprietorship, partnership, limited liability company (LLC), or corporation. Each structure has its own set of advantages and considerations, such as liability protection and tax implications. Additionally, it is important to obtain the necessary licenses and permits to operate your music production business legally. These may include business licenses, permits for operating a recording studio, and licenses for music distribution. Consulting with a business attorney or professional accountant can help you determine the most suitable business structure for your music production business and ensure you comply with all necessary licensing requirements.

Contracts and Agreements

Contracts and agreements play a critical role in the music production industry. When working with clients, it is essential to have clear and legally binding agreements to protect both parties' rights and responsibilities. These agreements may outline the terms of the recording and production services, payment terms, copyright ownership, and dispute resolution mechanisms. Working with an entertainment attorney can help you draft and review contracts and agreements specific to the music production industry. They can ensure that your interests are protected and that you have the necessary legal safeguards in place.

Insurance

Insurance is an important consideration for any business, including a music production business. It helps protect you and your assets from potential risks and liabilities that may arise during your work. This may include liability insurance, equipment insurance, and professional indemnity insurance. Consulting with an insurance agent who specializes in the music industry can help you identify the appropriate insurance coverage for your specific needs. They can help you understand the risks associated with your business and tailor an insurance policy that safeguards your interests.

Accounting and Financial Management

Effective financial management is crucial for the success and sustainability of your music production business. Keeping accurate financial records, tracking expenses and revenue, and planning for taxes are essential tasks. Hiring a professional accountant who is knowledgeable about the music industry can help you navigate the complexities of financial management. They can assist you with bookkeeping, tax planning, and financial forecasting, ensuring you have a solid financial foundation for your business.

Conclusion

Addressing the legal and business considerations of your music production business is essential for its long-term success. Protecting your intellectual property, choosing the right business structure, having solid contracts, obtaining appropriate insurance, and managing your finances are key components of running a legally compliant and sustainable business. Taking the time to understand and address these considerations will not only protect your business and your clients but also position you for growth and success in the music production industry.

Chapter 7: Marketing and Promotion Strategies

Hey there! Let's talk about something absolutely vital for your music production business: marketing and promotion. Without effective strategies, even the most talented producers can struggle to get noticed. In this chapter, we'll dive into various approaches to help you effectively market and promote your services to your target audience.

Understanding Your Target Audience

Before jumping into any marketing activities, it's crucial to have a solid grasp of who your target audience is. Think about the specific demographics, preferences, and needs of your potential clients. Conducting market research can be incredibly helpful here. This means gathering insights into the characteristics and behaviors of the people you want to reach. By doing this, you'll be able to fine-tune your marketing messages and select the most effective channels to connect with them.

Building a Strong Online Presence

In today's digital world, having a robust online presence is non-negotiable. Here are some key strategies to consider:

Website Development

First, you need a professional, user-friendly website. This site should showcase your services, highlight your portfolio, and include client testimonials. Make sure your website is optimized for search engines (SEO) to improve your visibility online. Think of it as your digital storefront – it needs to make a great first impression!

Social Media Marketing

Social media is your friend. Platforms like Facebook, Instagram, Twitter, and LinkedIn are perfect for connecting with your audience. Share regular updates, behind-the-scenes content, and client success stories. Engage with your followers by responding to comments and messages. This helps build a community around your brand.

Content Marketing

Content is king. Develop informative and valuable content related to music production and share it through blog posts, videos, podcasts, and infographics. This positions you as an industry expert and attracts potential clients. When people see the value in what you're sharing, they're more likely to trust you with their projects.

Email Marketing

Don't underestimate the power of a well-crafted email. Build an email list of potential clients and existing customers. Send out regular newsletters, updates, and special offers to keep them engaged and informed about your services. It's a direct line of communication that can drive repeat business and referrals.

Networking and Collaborations

The music industry thrives on connections. Attend industry events, conferences, and workshops to meet fellow producers, musicians, and other industry professionals. Networking can lead to collaborations and new client opportunities. Building relationships is key – you never know where your next big project might come from!

Online Advertising

Sometimes, you need to pay to play. Investing in online advertising can boost your visibility and help you reach a wider audience. Platforms like Google AdWords and social media advertising allow you to target specific demographics and interests, making your campaigns more effective.

Referral Programs

Word-of-mouth is incredibly powerful. Encourage satisfied clients to refer your services to their friends and colleagues through a referral program. Offer incentives like discounts or freebies to clients who bring in new business. This not only helps you generate new leads but also expands your client base through trusted recommendations.

Track and Analyze Results

It's essential to track and analyze the results of your marketing efforts. Use tools like Google Analytics to monitor website traffic, engagement, and conversions. This data will help you see which strategies are working and which need tweaking. Regularly reviewing this information ensures that you make informed decisions for future marketing campaigns.

Conclusion

Marketing and promotion are the lifeblood of your music production business. By understanding your target audience, building a strong online presence, networking, leveraging online advertising, and implementing referral programs, you can effectively market your services and attract a steady stream of clients. Regularly analyzing and refining your strategies will keep you ahead in the competitive music production industry.

So, get out there and start making some noise – in the best possible way! Happy marketing!

Chapter 8: Acquiring Clients and Building Relationships

Hey there! Now that you've got your music production services and pricing figured out, it's time to focus on one of the most important aspects of your business: acquiring clients and building strong relationships with them. A solid client base not only ensures a steady stream of work but also contributes to the long-term success and reputation of your business. In this chapter, we'll explore some effective strategies to help you attract clients and build lasting relationships.

Understanding Your Target Audience

Before you start reaching out to potential clients, it's essential to have a clear understanding of who you want to work with. Take the time to research and identify the types of artists, musicians, bands, or other professionals that align with your vision and services. Knowing your target audience will help you tailor your marketing and outreach efforts to attract the right clients.

Think about the genres of music you enjoy working with or the specific needs of different types of clients. Are you aiming to collaborate with indie artists, established bands, or even record labels? This knowledge will be your guiding star as you craft your strategies.

Building a Strong Online Presence

In today's digital age, having a strong online presence is absolutely crucial. Start by developing a professional website that showcases your work, services, and testimonials from satisfied clients. Make sure your website is user-friendly, visually appealing, and optimized for search engines. This will help potential clients find you more easily.

But don't stop at just having a website. Actively engage on social media platforms that cater to musicians and artists. Create compelling content related to music production, such as tips, behind-the-scenes insights, and examples of past projects. Regularly interact with your audience by responding to comments, messages, and inquiries promptly. This not only builds your online presence but also establishes you as an approachable and knowledgeable professional in the field.

Networking and Collaboration

Networking within the music industry can be one of the most effective ways to acquire clients. Attend industry events, conferences, and workshops where you can meet and connect with artists, managers, agents, and other industry professionals. Be proactive and approachable, showing genuine interest in their work and offering assistance where relevant.

Consider collaborating with artists or musicians on projects. This expands your portfolio and helps you tap into their existing fan base and network. Collaborative projects often lead to referrals and recommendations from artists who had a positive experience working with you.

Providing Exceptional Service and Quality

One of the most powerful ways to acquire clients is through word-of-mouth recommendations. By providing exceptional service and consistently delivering high-quality results, you'll naturally encourage clients to refer your services to others. Focus on exceeding client expectations, meeting deadlines, and being responsive to their needs and feedback.

Take the time to understand each client's unique vision and objectives for their music project. Tailor your approach and services to their specific requirements and preferences. Going the extra mile to ensure client satisfaction will not only lead to repeat business but also increase the likelihood of positive recommendations.

Implementing Referral Programs

Encourage your satisfied clients to refer your services to their contacts by implementing a referral program. Offer incentives such as discounts or free services for clients who refer new customers to your business. This not only rewards your existing clients but also serves as an additional motivator for them to spread the word about your services.

Tracking and Analyzing Results

To continuously improve your client acquisition strategies, it's important to track and analyze your results. Keep records of how clients found out about your business, whether through online channels, referrals, or other means. This data will help you identify which strategies are most effective in acquiring clients so you can allocate your resources accordingly.

Regularly review and analyze your client acquisition efforts to identify areas for improvement. Adjust your strategies based on the feedback and insights gained from client interactions and market trends. Stay updated on industry news and changes to ensure your client acquisition methods remain effective and relevant.

Conclusion

Acquiring clients and building strong relationships are essential aspects of running a successful music production business. By understanding your target audience, building a strong online presence, networking, providing exceptional service and quality, implementing referral programs, and tracking and analyzing results, you can effectively acquire and retain clients.

Focus on building genuine connections and delivering exceptional results. This will help you establish a strong client base and grow your music production business. Remember, your clients are the heartbeat of your business, so treat them with care and respect, and they will help your business thrive.

Chapter 9: Providing Exceptional Service and Quality

In the world of music production, providing exceptional service and quality is not just a nice-to-have; it's a necessity. These elements are the cornerstone of your success and growth. By consistently exceeding client expectations and delivering top-notch work, you can build a strong reputation and foster long-lasting relationships with your clients. Let's delve into the strategies and practices that will help you achieve this.

Understanding Client Needs and Expectations

To provide exceptional service and quality, you need to have a deep understanding of your clients' needs and expectations. This begins with effective communication and active listening. Take the time to thoroughly discuss their project requirements, objectives, and vision. Ask clarifying questions and seek feedback throughout the process to ensure you're on the right track. Understanding your client's vision is crucial to delivering a final product that meets or even exceeds their expectations.

Delivering on Time

Meeting deadlines is an essential aspect of providing exceptional service. Time management skills are key in the music production industry, where clients often have strict schedules and deadlines for their projects. Create a realistic timeline and production schedule. Ensure you have the necessary resources and team members to complete the work on time. If any potential delays or challenges arise, communicate these to your clients proactively and provide alternative solutions. This transparency helps build trust and shows your commitment to their project.

Attention to Detail

Attention to detail is a hallmark of exceptional service and quality. Ensure that your work is meticulous and error-free. This includes checking for any audio imperfections, properly aligning tracks, and ensuring a flawless mix and production. By consistently delivering high-quality work, you will build trust with your clients and establish yourself as a reliable and skilled music producer. The small details can make a big difference in the final product, so never overlook them.

Professionalism and Communication

Maintaining professionalism throughout all interactions with your clients is crucial. This includes promptly responding to emails and calls, being respectful and courteous, and keeping clients informed about the progress of their project. Effective communication is key to providing exceptional service. Clearly communicate your ideas, suggestions, and any necessary adjustments to ensure your clients are fully satisfied with the final product. A professional demeanor and clear communication can significantly enhance the client experience.

Continuous Education and Improvement

The music production industry is constantly evolving, with new technologies, techniques, and trends emerging regularly. To stay at the forefront of your field and provide exceptional service, it is important to invest in continuous education and improvement. Stay updated on the latest software applications, equipment advancements, and industry best practices. Attend workshops, conferences, and seminars relevant to your field to enhance your skills and knowledge. By continually improving, you can offer the latest and greatest to your clients, keeping your services fresh and relevant.

Soliciting Feedback and Learning from Mistakes

Feedback from clients is invaluable in improving your services and ensuring exceptional quality. Actively seek feedback at the completion of each project and encourage clients to provide honest evaluations. Take constructive criticism seriously and use it to enhance your skills and refine your processes. Additionally, learn from any mistakes or missteps that may occur during the course of a project. Use these experiences as opportunities for growth and improvement. A willingness to listen and adapt can set you apart from the competition.

Going Above and Beyond

Providing exceptional service and quality often requires going the extra mile for your clients. This may involve offering additional revisions, providing alternative options or solutions, or offering support and guidance beyond the scope of the project. By exceeding expectations and demonstrating your dedication to client satisfaction, you will build a strong reputation and attract repeat business and referrals. Going above and beyond shows clients that you truly care about their success and are willing to invest the extra effort to achieve it.

Conclusion

Providing exceptional service and quality is essential for success in the music production industry. By understanding client needs, delivering on time, paying attention to detail, maintaining professionalism, continuously improving, soliciting feedback, and going above and beyond, you can set yourself apart from the competition and build a thriving music production business. Remember that exceptional service and quality are the keys to client satisfaction and long-term success. Invest in these practices, and you'll see your business grow and flourish.

Chapter 10: Growing Your Music Production Business

Growing your music production business is essential for long-term success and achieving your entrepreneurial dreams. As the music industry evolves and technology continues to advance, it's crucial to adapt and expand your business to stay ahead of the competition and meet the changing needs of your clients. In this chapter, we'll explore key strategies and techniques to help you effectively grow your music production business.

1. Expand Your Services

One effective way to grow your music production business is to broaden your range of services. Think about offering additional services that complement what you already provide or cater to specific niches within the music industry. For instance, you could add services like songwriting, vocal coaching, arranging, or music licensing. By expanding your offerings, you can attract a wider client base and boost your revenue potential.

2. Develop Strategic Partnerships

Collaborating with other professionals in the music industry can be mutually beneficial. Look for opportunities to work with artists, songwriters, record labels, and other industry professionals. These collaborations can help you expand your network, gain exposure to new clients, and enhance your credibility. Building relationships with music venues, event organizers, and production companies can also be advantageous. By offering your services for live events, concerts, and music festivals, you can showcase your expertise and attract potential clients who may require your services in the future. Strategic partnerships can open doors to new opportunities and lead to referrals, ultimately boosting your business growth.

3. Build an Online Presence

In today's digital age, having a strong online presence is crucial for business growth. Start by creating a professional website that showcases your portfolio, services, and testimonials from satisfied clients. Optimize your website for search engines to improve visibility and attract organic traffic. Utilize social media platforms like Facebook, Instagram, Twitter, and LinkedIn to engage with your target audience, share updates, and promote your services. Regularly post content that showcases your expertise and provides value to your followers. Engage with your audience by responding to comments and messages promptly. Consider starting a blog or creating video content that provides valuable tips, tutorials, and insights related to music production. This can help position you as an industry expert and attract potential clients seeking your services.

4. Seek Referrals and Reviews

Word-of-mouth referrals and positive reviews can significantly impact the growth of your music production business. Encourage your satisfied clients to refer your services to their connections and offer incentives for successful referrals. Additionally, ask clients to provide feedback and testimonials that you can showcase on your website and social media platforms. Consider offering a discount or incentive for clients who leave a review on platforms like Google, Yelp, or specific music industry directories. Positive reviews and testimonials can build trust and credibility with potential clients, ultimately driving business growth.

5. Attend Industry Events and Networking Opportunities

Networking is essential for growth in the music production industry. Attend industry events such as music conferences, seminars, trade shows, and networking meetups. These events provide opportunities to connect with industry professionals, potential clients, and collaborators. Prepare a professional elevator pitch and have your business cards ready to exchange with contacts you meet. Follow up with your new connections after the event to nurture relationships and explore potential collaborations or business opportunities.

6. Invest in Professional Development

Continuously improving your skills and staying updated with industry trends is vital for the growth of your music production business. Invest in professional development by attending workshops, online courses, and masterclasses related to music production, sound engineering, and new technologies. Stay informed about emerging production techniques, software updates, and industry standards. Regularly practice and experiment with different production styles and techniques to enhance your skillset and offer unique services to your clients.

Conclusion

Growing your music production business requires dedication, strategic planning, and a commitment to providing exceptional services. By expanding your services, forming strategic partnerships, building an online presence, seeking referrals, attending industry events, and investing in professional development, you can position your business for long-term growth and success in the competitive music production industry. With the right strategies in place, you'll be well-equipped to navigate the ever-changing landscape and achieve your goals as a successful music producer.